BIBLE PROMISES FOR
Women

Inspiring | Educating | Creating | Entertaining

Brimming with creative inspiration, how-to projects, and useful information to enrich your everyday life, quarto.com is a favorite destination for those pursuing their interests and passions.

10 9 8 7 6 5 4 3 2 1

Chartwell titles are also available at discount for retail, wholesale, promotional, and bulk purchase. For details, contact the Special Sales Manager by email at specialsales@quarto.com or by mail at The Quarto Group, Attn: Special Sales Manager, 100 Cummings Center Suite 265D, Beverly, MA 01915, USA.

ISBN: 978-0-7858-4047-3

Library of Congress Control Number: 2021949409

Printed in China

Publisher: Wendy Friedman
Editorial Director: Betina Cochran
Creative Director: Pauline Molinari
Designer: Sue Boylan
Editor: Meredith Mennitt
Image credits: Shutterstock

BIBLE PROMISES FOR
Women

SPIRITUAL DEVOTIONS FOR EVERYDAY LIFE

chartwell
books

Contents

Every one of us has had those days.

THE ONES WHERE NO MATTER WHAT YOU DO, things go wrong. The car breaks down. You lose your phone. You are late for work and get that look from the boss. You get into an argument with a friend or family member and afterward you cannot remember how it started. Sometimes it can feel like the entire world is arrayed against you.

On days like that, many of us turn to the word of God. It is difficult to think of the situation you could face for which the Bible does not provide some form of guidance.

In *Bible Promises for Women*, you will find hundreds of quotations from the Holy Scripture. These selections are grouped into dozens of categories arranged by subject. The quotes range from the Psalms to the prophets to the preachings of Jesus Christ. Whether you are dealing with anger, sickness, or even plain old money problems, you know where to turn for guidance and support.

This way, when you are having one of those days, you can pick up this book, turn the page, be refreshed by the gift of His strength and wisdom, and face the day anew.

Blessings

AND I will make of thee a great nation, and I
will bless thee, and make thy name great;
and thou shalt be a blessing: And I will bless
them that bless thee, and curse him that
curseth thee: and in thee shall all families of
the earth be blessed.

~GENESIS 12:2–3

MAKE thy face to shine upon thy servant: save me for thy mercies' sake.

~*PSALMS 31:16*

NOW the God of hope fill you with all joy and peace in believing, that ye may abound in hope, through the power of the Holy Ghost.

~*ROMANS 15:13*

FOR Moses had said, Consecrate yourselves today to the LORD, even every man upon his son, and upon his brother; that he may bestow upon you a blessing this day.

~*EXODUS 32:29*

GRANT thee according to thine own heart, and fulfil all thy counsel.

~*PSALMS 20:4*

THE blessing of the LORD, it maketh rich, and he addeth no sorrow with it.

~*PROVERBS 10:22*

BLESS them which persecute you: bless, and curse not.

~*ROMANS 12:14*

BLESSED are they that keep his testimonies, and that seek him with the whole heart.

~*PSALMS 119:2*

AND God is able to make all grace abound toward you; that ye, always having all sufficiency in all things, may abound to every good work.

~*2 CORINTHIANS 9:8*

Jesus saith unto him, Thomas, because thou hast seen me, thou hast believed: blessed are they that have not seen, and yet have believed.

~JOHN 20:29

Calm

HE maketh the storm a calm, so that the waves thereof are still. Then are they glad because they be quiet; so he bringeth them unto their desired haven.

~*PSALMS 107:29–30*

BUT whoso hearkeneth unto me shall dwell safely, and shall be quiet from fear of evil.

~*PROVERBS 1:33*

IN the multitude of my thoughts within me thy comforts delight my soul.

~*PSALMS 94:19*

I, even I, am he that comforteth you.

~*ISAIAH 51:12*

~~~~~~

BE ye angry, and sin not: let not the sun go down upon your wrath: Neither give place to the devil.

~*EPHESIANS 4:26–27*

~~~~~~

HEAVINESS in the heart of man maketh it stoop: but a good mark maketh it glad.

~*PROVERBS 12:28*

~~~~~~

BE careful for nothing; but in every thing by prayer and supplication with thanksgiving let your requests be made known unto God. And the peace of God, which passeth all understanding, shall keep your hearts and minds through Christ Jesus.

~*PHILIPPIANS 4:6–7*

~~~~~~

AND he was in the hinder part of the ship, asleep on a pillow: and they awake him, and say unto him, Master, carest thou not that we perish? And he arose, and rebuked the wind, and said unto the sea, Peace, be still. And the wind ceased, and there was a great calm.

~MARK 4:38–39

TAKE therefore no thought for the morrow: for the morrow shall take thought for the things of itself. Sufficient unto the day is the evil thereof.

~MATTHEW 6:34

TRUST in the LORD with all thine heart, and lean not unto thine own understanding. In all thy ways acknowledge him, and he shall direct thy paths.

~PROVERBS 3:5–6

Caring

✦

...LET us not love in word, neither in tongue; but in deed and in truth.

~1 JOHN 3:18

THAT there should be no schism in the body; but that the members should have the same care one for another.

~1 CORINTHIANS 12:25

AND let us not be weary in well doing: for in due season we shall reap, if we faint not.

~GALATIANS 6:9

AND he looked up, and saw the rich men casting their gifts into the treasury. And he saw also a certain poor widow casting in thither two mites. And he said, Of a truth I say unto you, that this poor widow hath cast in more than they all: For all these have of their abundance cast in unto the offerings of God: but she of her penury hath cast in all the living that she had.

~*LUKE 21:1-4*

WITHHOLD not good from them to whom it is due, when it is in the power of thine hand to do it.

~PROVERBS 3:27

THEN shall the righteous answer him, saying, Lord, when saw we thee an hungred, and fed thee? or thirsty, and gave thee drink? When saw we thee a stranger, and took thee in? or naked, and clothed thee? Or when saw we thee sick, or in prison, and came unto thee? And the King shall answer and say unto them, Verily I say unto you, Inasmuch as ye have done it unto one of the least of these my brethren, ye have done it unto me.

~MATTHEW 25:37–40

And be ye kind
one to another,
tenderhearted,
forgiving one another,
even as God for
Christ's sake hath
forgiven you.

~EPHESIANS 4:32

Charity

HE that hath pity upon the poor lendeth unto
the Lord.

~PROVERBS 19:17

IT is more blessed to give than to receive.

~ACTS 20:35

BEHOLD, God is mighty, and despiseth not
any: he is mighty in strength and wisdom.
He preserveth not the life of the wicked: but
giveth right to the poor.

~JOB 36:5–6

EVERY man according as he purposeth in his heart, so let him give, not grudgingly, or of necessity: for God loveth a cheerful giver.

~2 CORINTHIANS 9:7

WHOSO stoppeth his ears at the cry of the poor, he also shall cry himself, but shall not be heard.

~PROVERBS 21:13

GIVE to him that asketh thee, and from him that would borrow of thee turn not thou away.

~MATTHEW 5:42

...FREELY ye have received, freely give.

~MATTHEW 10:8

BE not forgetful to entertain strangers:
for thereby some have entertained
angels unawares.

~HEBREWS 13:2

AND above all things have fervent charity
among yourselves: for charity shall cover the
multitude of sins.

~1 PETER 4:8

AND the people asked him, saying, What shall
we do then? He answereth and saith unto
them, He that hath two coats, let him impart
to him that hath none; and he that hath meat,
let him do likewise.

~LUKE 3:10 – 11

Children

CHILDREN are an heritage of the LORD: and the fruit of the womb is his reward.

~PSALMS 127:3

TAKE heed that ye despise not one of these little ones; for I say unto you, That in heaven their angels do always behold the face of my Father which is in heaven.

~MATTHEW 18:10

TRAIN up a child in the way he should go: and when he is old, he will not depart from it.

~PROVERBS 22:6

AND all thy children shall be taught of the
LORD; and great shall be the peace of
thy children.

~ISAIAH 54:13

THEN were there brought unto him little
children, that he should put his hands on
them, and pray: and the disciples rebuked
them. But Jesus said, Suffer little children,
and forbid them not, to come unto me: for of
such is the kingdom of heaven.

~MATTHEW 19:13–14

BUT thus saith the LORD, Even the captives
of the mighty shall be taken away, and the
prey of the terrible shall be delivered: for I
will contend with him that contendeth with
thee, and I will save thy children.

~ISAIAH 49:25

BY this we know that we love the children of God, when we love God, and keep his commandments.

~1 JOHN 5:2

I have no greater joy than to hear that my children walk in truth.

~3 JOHN 1:4

EVEN a child is known by his doings, whether his work be pure, and whether it be right.

~PROVERBS 20:11

Only take heed to thyself, and keep thy soul diligently, lest thou forget the things which thine eyes have seen, and lest they depart from thy heart all the days of thy life: but teach them thy sons, and thy sons' sons.

~DEUTERONOMY 4:9

Compassion

...BE ye all of one mind, having compassion one of another, love as brethren, be pitiful, be courteous.

~1 PETER 3:8

SHE openeth her mouth with wisdom; and in her tongue is the law of kindness.

~PROVERBS 31:26

REJOICE with them that do rejoice, and weep with them that weep.

~ROMANS 12:15

...OPPRESS not the widow, nor the fatherless, the stranger, nor the poor; and let none of you imagine evil against his brother in your heart.

~ZECHARIAH 7:10

BUT love ye your enemies, and do good, and lend, hoping for nothing again; and your reward shall be great, and ye shall be the children of the Highest: for he is kind unto the unthankful and to the evil.

~LUKE 6:35

BUT when he saw the multitudes, he was moved with compassion on them, because they fainted, and were scattered abroad, as sheep having no shepherd.

~MATTHEW 9:36

Forbearing
one another,
and forgiving
one another,
if any man
have a quarrel
against any:
even as Christ
forgave you, so
also do ye.

~*COLOSSIANS 3:13*

THE LORD is merciful and gracious, slow to anger, and plenteous in mercy.

~*PSALMS 103:8*

AS we have therefore opportunity, let us do good unto all men.

~*GALATIANS 6:10*

AND though I bestow all my goods to feed the poor, and though I give my body to be burned, and have not charity, it profiteth me nothing.

~*1 CORINTHIANS 13:3*

Confidence

BELOVED, if our heart condemn us not, then
have we confidence toward God.

~1 JOHN 3:21

IN the fear of the LORD is strong confidence:
and his children shall have a place of refuge.

~PROVERBS 14:26

HAVE not I commanded thee? Be strong and
of a good courage; be not afraid, neither be
thou dismayed: for the LORD thy God is with
thee whithersoever thou goest.

~JOSHUA 1:9

SOME trust in chariots, and some in horses:
but we will remember the name of the
LORD our God.

~PSALMS 20:7

AND he said unto me, My grace is sufficient
for thee: for my strength is made perfect in
weakness. Most gladly therefore will I rather
glory in my infirmities, that the power of
Christ may rest upon me.

~2 CORINTHIANS 12:9

FOR the LORD shall be thy confidence, and
shall keep thy foot from being taken.

~PROVERBS 3:26

THEN shalt thou walk in thy way safely, and
thy foot shall not stumble.

~PROVERBS 3:23

AND I was with you in weakness, and in fear, and in much trembling. And my speech and my preaching was not with enticing words of man's wisdom, but in demonstration of the Spirit and of power: That your faith should not stand in the wisdom of men, but in the power of God.

~1 CORINTHIANS 2:3–5

LET us therefore come boldly unto the throne of grace, that we may obtain mercy, and find grace to help in time of need.

~HEBREWS 4:16

Though an host
should encamp
against me, my heart
shall not fear: though
war should rise
against me, in this will
I be confident.

~PSALMS 27:3

Conflict

IN what place therefore ye hear the sound of the trumpet, resort ye thither unto us: our God shall fight for us.

~NEHEMIAH 4:20

A soft answer turneth away wrath: but grievous words stir up anger.

~PROVERBS 15:1

BUT foolish and unlearned questions avoid, knowing that they do gender strifes.

~2 TIMOTHY 2:23

DARE any of you, having a matter against another, go to law before the unjust, and not before the saints?

~*1 CORINTHIANS 6:1*

BE merciful unto me, O God: for man would swallow me up; he fighting daily oppresseth me.

~*PSALMS 56:1*

THE LORD shall fight for you, and ye shall hold your peace.

~*EXODUS 14:14*

THOU shalt not avenge, nor bear any grudge
against the children of thy people, but
thou shalt love thy neighbour as thyself: I
am the LORD.

~*LEVITICUS 19:18*

FOR where envying and strife is, there is
confusion and every evil work. But the
wisdom that is from above is first pure, then
peaceable, gentle, and easy to be intreated,
full of mercy and good fruits, without
partiality, and without hypocrisy. And the
fruit of righteousness is sown in peace of
them that make peace. From whence come
wars and fightings among you?

~*JAMES 3:16 – 4:1*

DEPART from evil, and do good; seek peace,
and pursue it.

~*PSALMS 34:14*

A time to rend
and a time to sew;
a time to keep
silence, and a
time to speak. A
time to love, and
a time to hate; a
time of war, and a
time of peace.

~ECCLESIASTES 3:7–8

Dependence

BUT she that liveth in pleasure is dead while she liveth.

~1 TIMOTHY 5:6

FOR God hath not given us the spirit of fear; but of power, and of love, and of a sound mind.

~2 TIMOTHY 1:7

IF the Son therefore shall make you free, ye shall be free indeed.

~JOHN 8:36

SUBMIT yourselves therefore to God. Resist the devil, and he will flee from you.

~JAMES 4:7

~~~~~~~~~~~~~~~~~~~~~~~~~~~~~~~~~~~~~~

FOR all that is in the world, the lust of the flesh, and the lust of the eyes, and the pride of life, is not of the Father, but is of the world.

~1 JOHN 2:16

~~~~~~~~~~~~~~~~~~~~~~~~~~~~~~~~~~~~~~

BE sober, be vigilant; because your adversary the devil, as a roaring lion, walketh about, seeking whom he may devour.

~1 PETER 5:8

~~~~~~~~~~~~~~~~~~~~~~~~~~~~~~~~~~~~~~

KNOW ye not that ye are the temple of God, and that the Spirit of God dwelleth in you?

~1 CORINTHIANS 3:16

~~~~~~~~~~~~~~~~~~~~~~~~~~~~~~~~~~~~~~

THEY gave him vinegar to drink mingled with gall: and when he had tasted thereof, he would not drink.

~MATTHEW 27:34

THE priest and the prophet have erred through strong drink, they are swallowed up of wine, they are out of the way through strong drink; they err in vision, they stumble in judgment.

~ISAIAH 28:7

NOR thieves, nor covetous, nor drunkards, nor revilers, nor extortioners, shall inherit the kingdom of God. And such were some of you: but ye are washed, but ye are sanctified, but ye are justified in the name of the Lord Jesus, and by the Spirit of our God.

~1 CORINTHIANS 6:10–11

ALL the labour of man is for his mouth, and
yet the appetite is not filled.

~*ECCLESIASTES 6:7*

WINE is a mocker, strong drink is raging: and
whosoever is deceived thereby is not wise.

~*PROVERBS 20:1*

Discipline

DESIRE not the night, when people are cut off in their place. Take heed, regard not iniquity: for this hast thou chosen rather than affliction.

~JOB 36:20–21

SLOTHFULNESS casteth into a deep sleep; and an idle soul shall suffer hunger.

~PROVERBS 19:15

BUT the end of all things is at hand: be ye therefore sober, and watch unto prayer.

~1 PETER 4:7

FOR the commandment is a lamp; and the law is light; and reproofs of instruction are the way of life.

~PROVERBS 6:23

BUT when we are judged, we are chastened of the Lord, that we should not be condemned with the world.

~1 CORINTHIANS 11:32

LET no corrupt communication proceed out of your mouth, but that which is good to the use of edifying.

~EPHESIANS 4:29

THE soul of the sluggard desireth, and hath nothing.

~PROVERBS 13:4

BECAUSE strait is the gate, and narrow is the way, which leadeth unto life, and few there be that find it.

~MATTHEW 7:14

BUT speak thou the things which become sound doctrine: That the aged men be sober, grave, temperate, sound in faith, in charity, in patience. The aged women likewise, that they be in behaviour as becometh holiness.

~TITUS 2:1–3

NOW no chastening for the present seemeth to be joyous, but grievous: nevertheless afterward it yieldeth the peaceable fruit of righteousness unto them which are exercised thereby.

~HEBREWS 12:11

Doubt

AND immediately Jesus stretched forth his hand, and caught him, and said unto him, O thou of little faith, wherefore didst thou doubt?

~MATTHEW 14:31

AND he said unto them, Why are ye troubled? and why do thoughts arise in your hearts?

~LUKE 24:38

AND he said unto them, Why are ye so fearful? how is it that ye have no faith?

~MARK 4:40

SO then faith cometh by hearing, and hearing by the word of God.

~ROMANS 10:17

FOR verily I say unto you, That whosoever shall say unto this mountain, Be thou removed, and be thou cast into the sea; and shall not doubt in his heart, but shall believe that those things which he saith shall come to pass; he shall have whatsoever he saith.

~MARK 11:23

JESUS answered and said unto them, Verily I say unto you, If ye have faith, and doubt not, ye shall not only do this which is done to the fig tree, but also if ye shall say unto this mountain, Be thou removed, and be thou cast into the sea; it shall be done.

~MATTHEW 21:21

BUT let him ask in faith, nothing wavering. For he that wavereth is like a wave of the sea driven with the wind and tossed.

~JAMES 1:6

~~~~~~~~~~~~~~~~~~~~~~~~~~~~~~~~~~

AND when they saw him, they worshipped him: but some doubted. And Jesus came and spake unto them, saying, All power is given unto me in heaven and in earth.

~MATTHEW 28:17–18

~~~~~~~~~~~~~~~~~~~~~~~~~~~~~~~~~~

IF then God so clothe the grass, which is to day in the field, and to morrow is cast into the oven; how much more will he clothe you, O ye of little faith? And seek not ye what ye shall eat, or what ye shall drink, neither be ye of doubtful mind.

~LUKE 12:28–29

THEN saith he to Thomas, Reach hither thy finger, and behold my hands; and reach hither thy hand, and thrust it into my side: and be not faithless, but believing. And Thomas answered and said unto him, My LORD and my God. Jesus saith unto him, Thomas, because thou hast seen me, thou hast believed: blessed are they that have not seen, and yet have believed.

~JOHN 20:27–29

Encouragement

THOU hast also given me the shield of
thy salvation: and thy gentleness hath
made me great.

~2 SAMUEL 22:36

THE LORD will give strength unto his people;
the LORD will bless his people with peace.

~PSALMS 29:11

SO that we may boldly say, The Lord is my
helper, and I will not fear what man shall
do unto me.

~HEBREWS 13:6

BUT the Lord is faithful, who shall stablish
you, and keep you from evil.

~*2 THESSALONIANS 3:3*

THESE things have I written unto you that
believe on the name of the Son of God; that ye
may know that ye have eternal life, and that ye
may believe on the name of the Son of God.

~*1 JOHN 5:13*

TAKE my yoke upon you, and learn of me; for I am meek and lowly in heart: and ye shall find rest unto your souls.

~MATTHEW 11:28

MANY daughters have done virtuously, but thou excellest them all. Favour is deceitful, and beauty is vain: but a woman that feareth the LORD, she shall be praised. Give her of the fruit of her hands; and let her own works praise her in the gates.

~PROVERBS 31:29–31

AND that, knowing the time, that now it is high time to awake out of sleep: for now is our salvation nearer than when we believed. The night is far spent, the day is at hand: let us therefore cast off the works of darkness, and let us put on the armour of light.

~ROMANS 13:11–12

IF I ascend up into heaven, thou art there:
if I make my bed in hell, behold, thou art there.
If I take the wings of the morning, and dwell
in the uttermost parts of the sea; Even there
shall thy hand lead me, and thy right hand
shall hold me. If I say, Surely the darkness
shall cover me; even the night shall be light
about me.

~PSALMS 139:8–12

FOR the which cause I also suffer these
things: nevertheless I am not ashamed:
for I know whom I have believed, and am
persuaded that he is able to keep that which I
have committed unto him against that day.

~2 TIMOTHY 1:12

DELIGHT thyself also in the LORD: and he
shall give thee the desires of thine heart.

~PSALMS 37:4

Faith

NOW faith is the substance of things hoped for, the evidence of things not seen.

~PSALMS 11:1

BUT, beloved, be not ignorant of this one thing, that one day is with the Lord as a thousand years, and a thousand years as one day.

~2 PETER 3:8

...FAITH is the substance of things hoped for, the evidence of things not seen.

~HEBREWS 11:1

TEACH me, O LORD, the way of thy statutes;
and I shall keep it unto the end.

~PSALMS 119:33

I can do all things through Christ which
strengtheneth me.

~PHILIPPIANS 4:13

EVERY word of God is pure: he is a shield unto
them that put their trust in him.

~PROVERBS 30:5

I have not hid thy righteousness within my
heart; I have declared thy faithfulness
and thy salvation: I have not concealed thy
loving kindness and thy truth from the great
congregation.

~PSALMS 40:10

THESE shall make war with the Lamb, and the Lamb shall overcome them: for he is Lord of lords, and King of kings: and they that are with him are called, and chosen, and faithful.

~REVELATIONS 17:14

LET us draw near with a true heart in full assurance of faith, having our hearts sprinkled from an evil conscience, and our bodies washed with pure water.

~HEBREWS 10:22

FOR he hath delivered me out of all trouble: and mine eye hath seen his desire upon mine enemies.

~PSALMS 54:7

It is of the LORD's
mercies that we
are not consumed,
because his
compassions fail
not. They are new
every morning: great
is thy faithfulness.

~LAMENTATIONS 3:22–23

Family

AND HOME

CHILDREN, obey your parents in all things: for this is well pleasing unto the Lord.

~COLOSSIANS 3:20

BETTER is a dinner of herbs where love is, than a stalled ox and hatred therewith.

~PROVERBS 15:17

A wise son maketh a glad father: but a foolish man despiseth his mother.

~PROVERBS 15:20

BUILD ye houses, and dwell in them; and plant gardens, and eat the fruit of them.

~JEREMIAH 29:5

THROUGH wisdom is an house builded; and by understanding it is established.

~PROVERBS 24:3

THEREFORE shall a man leave his father and his mother, and shall cleave unto his wife: and they shall be one flesh.

~GENESIS 2:24

AND he will love thee, and bless thee, and multiply thee: he will also bless the fruit of thy womb.

~DEUTERONOMY 7:13

And my people
shall dwell in
a peaceable
habitation, and
in sure dwellings,
and in quiet
resting places.

~ISAIAH 32:18

EVERY wise woman buildeth her house: but the foolish plucketh it down with her hands.

~PROVERBS 14:1

BELIEVE on the Lord Jesus Christ, and thou shalt be saved, and thy house.

~ACTS 16:31

Fear
AND WORRIES

WHAT time I am afraid, I will trust in thee.
In God I will praise his word, in God have I
put my trust; I will not fear what flesh can
do unto me.

~PSALMS 56:3–4

THEREFORE I say unto you, Take no thought
for your life, what ye shall eat, or what ye
shall drink; nor yet for your body, what ye
shall put on. Is not the life more than meat,
and the body than raiment?

~MATTHEW 6:25

FEAR not, little flock; for it is your Father's good pleasure to give you the kingdom.

~*LUKE 12:32*

AND he saith unto them, Why are ye fearful, O ye of little faith? Then he arose, and rebuked the winds and the sea; and there was a great calm.

~*MATTHEW 8:26*

THE LORD is my light and my salvation; whom shall I fear? the LORD is the strength of my life; of whom shall I be afraid?

~*PSALMS 27:1*

GOD is our refuge and strength a very present help in trouble.

~*PSALMS 46:1*

ABIDE thou with me, fear not: for he that seeketh my life seeketh thy life: but with me thou shalt be in safeguard.

~1 SAMUEL 22:23

AND the LORD, he it is that doth go before thee; he will be with thee, he will not fail thee, neither forsake thee: fear not, neither be dismayed.

~1 DEUTERONOMY 31:8

LET not your heart be troubled: ye believe in God, believe also in me.

~JOHN 14:1

And the angel
said unto them,
Fear not: for,
behold, I bring
you good tidings
of great joy,
which shall be to
all people.

~LUKE 2:10

Forgiveness

I will not cause mine anger to fall upon you: for I am merciful, saith the LORD, and I will not keep anger for ever.

~JEREMIAH 3:12

AND forgive us our sins; for we also forgive every one that is indebted to us. And lead us not into temptation; but deliver us from evil.

~LUKE 11:4

FOR if ye forgive men their trespasses, your heavenly Father will also forgive you.

~MATTHEW 6:14

AND when ye stand praying, forgive, if ye have ought against any: that your Father also which is in heaven may forgive you your trespasses.

~MARK 11:25

TAKE heed to yourselves: If thy brother trespass against thee, rebuke him; and if he repent, forgive him. And if he trespass against thee seven times in a day, and seven times in a day turn again to thee, saying, I repent; thou shalt forgive him.

~LUKE 17:3–4

BUT I say unto you which hear, Love your enemies, do good to them which hate you, Bless them that curse you, and pray for them which despitefully use you.

~LUKE 6:27–28

FOR thou, Lord, art good, and ready to forgive; and plenteous in mercy unto all them that call upon thee.

~*PSALMS 86:5*

BRETHREN, I count not myself to have apprehended: but this one thing I do, forgetting those things which are behind, and reaching forth unto those things which are before.

~*EPHESIANS 3:13*

...THIS one thing I do, forgetting those things which are behind, and reaching forth unto those things which are before.

~*PHILIPPIANS 3:13*

WHEREFORE I say unto thee, Her sins, which are many, are forgiven; for she loved much: but to whom little is forgiven, the same loveth little.

~*LUKE 7:47*

Friendship

AND the Lord turned the captivity of Job,
when he prayed for his friends: also the Lord
gave Job twice as much as he had before.

~JOB 42:10

WHEREFORE comfort yourselves together,
and edify one another, even as also ye do.

~1 THESSALONIANS 5:11

WITHOUT counsel purposes are disappointed:
but in the multitude of counsellors they are
established.

~PROVERBS 15:22

HENCEFORTH I call you not servants; for the servant knoweth not what his lord doeth: but I have called you friends; for all things that I have heard of my Father I have made known unto you.

~JOHN 15:15

A friend loveth at all times.

~PROVERBS 17:17

TO him that is afflicted pity should be shewed from his friend.

~JOB 6:14

AND let us consider one another to provoke unto love and to good works.

~HEBREWS 10:24

...INTREAT me not to leave thee, or to return from following after thee: for whither thou goest, I will go; and where thou lodgest, I will lodge: thy people shall be my people, and thy God my God.

~RUTH 1:16

FAITHFUL are the wounds of a friend.

~PROVERBS 27:6

Frustration

AND ANGER

YE have heard that it was said by them of old time, Thou shalt not kill; and whosoever shall kill shall be in danger of the judgment. But I say unto you, That whosoever is angry with his brother without a cause shall be in danger of the judgment.

~PSALMS 5:21–22

LET not the anger of my lord wax hot: thou knowest the people, that they are set on mischief.

~EXODUS 32:22

MAKE no friendship with an angry man; and
with a furious man thou shalt not go.

~PROVERBS 22:24

HE that is slow to wrath is of great
understanding: but he that is hasty of spirit
exalteth folly.

~PROVERBS 14:29

CEASE from anger, and forsake wrath: fret
not thyself in any wise to do evil.

~PSALMS 37:8

BEHOLD, I have taken out of thine hand the
cup of trembling, even the dregs of the cup of
my fury; thou shalt no more drink it again.

~ISAIAH 51:22

IF thou bring thy gift to the altar, and there rememberest that thy brother hath ought against thee; Leave there thy gift before the altar, and go thy way; first be reconciled to thy brother, and then come and offer thy gift.

~*MATTHEW 5:23–24*

THE LORD is slow to anger, and great in power.

~*NAHUM 1:3*

IT is an honour for a man to cease from strife: but every fool will be meddling.

~*PROVERBS 20:3*

Wherefore,
my beloved
brethren, let
every man be
swift to hear,
slow to speak,
slow to wrath.

~JAMES 1:19

Generosity

⧬

BUT the stranger that dwelleth with you shall be unto you as one born among you, and thou shalt love him as thyself; for ye were strangers in the land of Egypt: I am the LORD your God.

~LEVITICUS 19:34

BEAR ye one another's burdens, and so fulfil the law of Christ.

~GALATIANS 6:2

SELL that ye have, and give alms.

~LUKE 12:33

AND he said unto them, Take heed, and beware of covetousness: for a man's life consisteth not in the abundance of the things which he possesseth.

~LUKE 12:15

~~~~~~~~~~~~~~~~~~~~~~~~~~~~~~~~~~~

THERE is that scattereth, and yet increaseth; and there is that withholdeth more than is meet, but it tendeth to poverty.

~PROVERBS 11:24

~~~~~~~~~~~~~~~~~~~~~~~~~~~~~~~~~~~

AND when ye reap the harvest of your land, thou shalt not wholly reap the corners of thy field, neither shalt thou gather the gleanings of thy harvest. And thou shalt not glean thy vineyard, neither shalt thou gather every grape of thy vineyard; thou shalt leave them for the poor and stranger.

~LEVITICUS 19:9–10

~~~~~~~~~~~~~~~~~~~~~~~~~~~~~~~~~~~

Pure religion and
undefiled before
God and the
Father is this, To
visit the fatherless
and widows in
their affliction,
and to keep
himself unspotted
from the world.

~JAMES 1:27

JESUS said unto him, If thou wilt be perfect, go and sell that thou hast, and give to the poor, and thou shalt have treasure in heaven: and come and follow me.

~MATTHEW 19:21

IF a brother or sister be naked, and destitute of daily food, And one of you say unto them, Depart in peace, be ye warmed and filled; notwithstanding ye give them not those things which are needful to the body; what doth it profit?

~JAMES 2:15–16

BELOVED, I wish above all things that thou mayest prosper and be in health, even as thy soul prospereth.

~3 JOHN 1:2

God's Love

THE LORD is my portion, saith my soul; therefore will I hope in him.

~LAMENTATIONS 3:24

BUT God, who is rich in mercy, for his great love wherewith he loved us, Even when we were dead in sins, hath quickened us together with Christ, (by grace ye are saved;) And hath raised us up together, and made us sit together in heavenly places in Christ Jesus: That in the ages to come he might shew the exceeding riches of his grace in his kindness toward us through Christ Jesus.

~EPHESIANS 2:4–7

THE LORD thy God in the midst of thee is mighty; he will save, he will rejoice over thee with joy; he will rest in his love, he will joy over thee with singing.

~*ZEPHANIAH 3:17*

GOD saw that it was good.

~*GENESIS 1:10*

THAT Christ may dwell in your hearts by faith; that ye, being rooted and grounded in love. May be able to comprehend with all saints what is the breadth, and length, and depth, and height. And to know the love of Christ, which passeth knowledge, that ye might be filled with all the fulness of God.

~EPHESIANS 3:17–19

AND the Lord direct your hearts into the love of God, and into the patient waiting for Christ.

~2 THESSALONIANS 3:5

HOW excellent is thy lovingkindness, O God! therefore the children of men put their trust under the shadow of thy wings.

~PSALMS 36:7

WE love him, because he first loved us.

~1 JOHN 4:19

FOR the Father himself loveth you, because ye have loved me, and have believed that I came out from God.

~JOHN 16:27

Grace

FOR sin shall not have dominion over you: for
ye are not under the law, but under grace.

~*ROMANS 6:14*

THE LORD bless thee, and keep thee: The
LORD make his face shine upon thee, and
be gracious unto thee: The LORD lift up his
countenance upon thee, and give thee peace.

~*NUMBERS 6:24–26*

SURELY he scorneth the scorners: but he
giveth grace unto the lowly.

~*PROVERBS 3:34*

AND Jacob said, Nay, I pray thee, if now I have found grace in thy sight, then receive my present at my hand: for therefore I have seen thy face, as though I had seen the face of God, and thou wast pleased with me.

~GENESIS 33:10

AND let the beauty of the LORD our God be upon us: and establish thou the work of our hands upon us; yea, the work of our hands establish thou it.

~PSALMS 90:17

FOR if ye turn again unto the LORD, your brethren and your children shall find compassion before them that lead them captive, so that they shall come again into this land: for the LORD your God is gracious and merciful, and will not turn away his face from you, if ye return unto him.

~2 CHRONICLES 30:9

WHEREFORE gird up the loins of your mind, be sober, and hope to the end for the grace that is to be brought unto you at the revelation of Jesus Christ.

~1 PETER 1:13

LET the wicked forsake his way, and the unrighteous man his thoughts: and let him return unto the LORD, and he will have mercy upon him; and to our God, for he will abundantly pardon.

~ISAIAH 55:7

And therefore will the LORD wait, that he may be gracious unto you, and therefore will he be exalted, that he may have mercy upon you: for the LORD is a God of judgment: blessed are all they that wait for him.

~ISAIAH 30:18

Gratitude
TO AND FOR OTHERS

CEASE not to give thanks for you, making mention of you in my prayers.

~EPHESIANS 1:16

WE give thanks to God always for you all, making mention of you in our prayers.

~1 THESSALONIANS 1:2

I thank my God, making mention of thee always in my prayers.

~PHILEMON 1:4

... I thank my God through Jesus Christ
for you all, that your faith is spoken of
throughout the whole world.

~ROMANS 1:8

I thank God, whom I serve from my
forefathers with pure conscience, that
without ceasing I have remembrance of thee
in my prayers night and day; Greatly desiring
to see thee, being mindful of thy tears, that I
may be filled with joy.

~2 TIMOTHY 1:3–4

I thank my God upon every remembrance of
you, Always in every prayer of mine for you all
making request with joy, For your fellowship in
the gospel from the first day until now.

~PHILIPPIANS 1:3–5

I thank my God always on your behalf, for the grace of God which is given you by Jesus Christ; That in every thing ye are enriched by him, in all utterance, and in all knowledge.

~1 CORINTHIANS 1:4–5

THE LORD recompense thy work, and a full reward be given thee of the LORD God of Israel, under whose wings thou art come to trust.

~RUTH 2:12

And now the LORD shew kindness and truth unto you: and I also will requite you this kindness, because ye have done this thing.

-2 SAMUEL 2:6

Grieving

THE wicked is driven away in his wickedness: but the righteous hath hope in his death.

~PROVERBS 14:32

THE LORD is good, a strong hold in the day of trouble; and he knoweth them that trust in him.

~NAHUM 1:7

HE healeth the broken in heart, and bindeth up their wounds.

~PSALMS 147:3

BLESSED are they that mourn: for they shall
be comforted.

~MATTHEW 5:4

THE righteous cry, and the LORD heareth,
and delivereth them out of all their troubles.
The LORD is nigh unto them that are of a
broken heart; and saveth such as be of a
contrite spirit. Many are the afflictions of the
righteous: but the LORD delivereth him out
of them all.

~PSALMS 34:17–19

BUT the God of all grace, who hath called
us unto his eternal glory by Christ Jesus,
after that ye have suffered a while, make you
perfect, stablish, strengthen, settle you.

~1 PETER 5:10

For this God is
our God for ever
and ever: he will
be our guide even
unto death.

~PSALMS 48:14

AND God shall wipe away all tears from their eyes; and there shall be no more death, neither sorrow, nor crying, neither shall there be any more pain: for the former things are passed away.

~REVELATIONS 21:4

I will turn their mourning into joy, and will comfort them, and make them rejoice from their sorrow.

~JEREMIAH 31:13

IT is better to go to the house of mourning, than to go to the house of feasting: for that is the end of all men; and the living will lay it to his heart. Sorrow is better than laughter: for by the sadness of the countenance the heart is made better. The heart of the wise is in the house of mourning; but the heart of fools is in the house of mirth.

~ECCLESIASTES 7:2–4

Hardship

AND ye shall seek me, and find me, when ye shall search for me with all your heart.

~JEREMIAH 29:13

THIS know also, that in the last days perilous times shall come.

~2 TIMOTHY 3:1

BUT rejoice, inasmuch as ye are partakers of Christ's sufferings; that, when his glory shall be revealed, ye may be glad also with exceeding joy.

~PETER 4:13

BUT the salvation of the righteous is of the LORD: he is their strength in the time of trouble.

~PSALMS 37:39

THE LORD also will be a refuge for the oppressed, a refuge in times of trouble. And they that know thy name will put their trust in thee: for thou, LORD, hast not forsaken them that seek thee.

~PSALMS 9:9–10

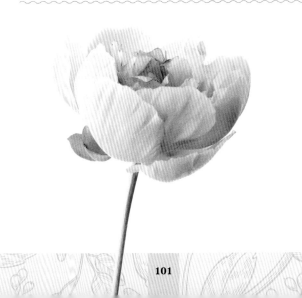

HAVE mercy upon me, O LORD, for I am in trouble: mine eye is consumed with grief, yea, my soul and my belly. For my life is spent with grief, and my years with sighing: my strength faileth because of mine iniquity, and my bones are consumed.

~PSALMS 31:9–10

MY flesh and my heart faileth: but God is the strength of my heart, and my portion for ever.

~PSALMS 73:26

WHEREIN ye greatly rejoice, though now
for a season, if need be, ye are in heaviness
through manifold temptations. That the trial
of your faith, being much more precious than
of gold that perisheth, though it be tried with
fire, might be found unto praise and honour
and glory at the appearing of Jesus Christ.

~1 PETER 1:6–7

THESE things I have spoken unto you, that in
me ye might have peace. In the world ye shall
have tribulation: but be of good cheer; I have
overcome the world.

~JOHN 16:33

FEAR thou not; for I am with thee: be not
dismayed; for I am thy God: I will strengthen
thee; yea, I will help thee; yea, I will uphold
thee with the right hand of my righteousness.

~ISAIAH 41:10

Healing

HAVE mercy upon me, O LORD; for I am weak:
O LORD, heal me; for my bones are vexed.

~PSALMS 6:2

HEAL me, O LORD, and I shall be healed;
save me, and I shall be saved: for thou art
my praise.

~JEREMIAH 17:14

FOR I will restore health unto thee, and I will
heal thee of thy wounds, saith the LORD...

~JEREMIAH 30:17

IS any sick among you? Let him call for the elders of the church; and let them pray over him, anointing him with oil in the name of the Lord.

~*JAMES 5:14*

O LORD my God, I cried unto thee, and thou hast healed me.

~*PSALMS 30:2*

BUT when Jesus heard it, he answered him, saying, Fear not: believe only, and she shall be made whole.

~*LUKE 8:50*

HE giveth power to the faint; and to them that have no might he increaseth strength.

~*ISAIAH 40:29*

A merry heart doeth good like a medicine: but a broken spirit drieth the bones.

~PROVERBS 17:22

AND ye shall serve the LORD your God, and he shall bless thy bread, and thy water; and I will take sickness away from the midst of thee.

~EXODUS 23:25

THEN they cry unto the LORD in their trouble, and he saveth them out of their distresses. He sent his word, and healed them, and delivered them from their destructions.

~PSALMS 107:19–20

...AND he received them, and spake unto them of the kingdom of God, and healed them that had need of healing.

~LUKE 9:11

Heaven

IN the beginning God created the heaven and
the earth.

~GENESIS 1:1

FROM that time Jesus began to preach, and
to say, Repent: for the kingdom of heaven
is at hand.

~MATTHEW 4:17

GOD looked down from heaven upon the
children of men, to see if there were any that
did understand, that did seek God.

~PSALMS 53:2

BUT as it is written, Eye hath not seen, nor ear heard, neither have entered into the heart of man, the things which God hath prepared for them that love him.

~1 CORINTHIANS 2:9

...THEREFORE hear the word of the LORD; I saw the LORD sitting upon his throne, and all the host of heaven standing on his right hand and on his left.

~2 CHRONICLES 18:18

AND I saw the dead, small and great, stand before God; and the books were opened: and another book was opened, which is the book of life: and the dead were judged out of those things which were written in the books, according to their works.

~REVELATIONS 20:12

AND I saw a new heaven and a new earth:
for the first heaven and the first earth were
passed away; and there was no more sea.
And I John saw the holy city, new Jerusalem,
coming down from God out of heaven,
prepared as a bride adorned for her husband.
And I heard a great voice out of heaven
saying, Behold, the tabernacle of God is with
men, and he will dwell with them, and they
shall be his people, and God himself shall be
with them, and be their God.

~REVELATIONS 21:1–4

IN my Father's house are many mansions:
if it were not so, I would have told you. I go
to prepare a place for you. And if I go and
prepare a place for you, I will come again,
and receive you unto myself; that where I am,
there ye may be also.

~JOHN 14:2–3

AND he carried me away in the spirit to a great and high mountain, and shewed me that great city, the holy Jerusalem, descending out of heaven from God, Having the glory of God: and her light was like unto a stone most precious, even like a jasper stone, clear as crystal.

~REVELATIONS 21:10–11

LAY not up for yourselves treasures upon earth, where moth and rust doth corrupt, and where thieves break through and steal: But lay up for yourselves treasures in heaven, where neither moth nor rust doth corrupt, and where thieves do not break through nor steal: For where your treasure is, there will your heart be also.

~MATTHEW 6:19–21

Honesty

PROVIDING for honest things, not only in the sight of the Lord, but also in the sight of men.

~*2 CORINTHIANS 8:21*

A wicked doer giveth heed to false lips; and a liar giveth ear to a naughty tongue.

~*PROVERBS 17:4*

HE that saith, I know him, and keepeth not his commandments, is a liar, and the truth is not in him.

~*1 JOHN 2:4*

LYING lips are abomination to the LORD: but
they that deal truly are his delight.

~PROVERBS 12:22

~~~~~~~~~~~~~~~~~~~~~~~~~~

LET the lying lips be put to silence;
which speak grievous things proudly and
contemptuously against the righteous.

~PSALMS 31:18

~~~~~~~~~~~~~~~~~~~~~~~~~~

BEHOLD, ye trust in lying words, that
cannot profit.

~JEREMIAH 7:8

~~~~~~~~~~~~~~~~~~~~~~~~~~

THE integrity of the upright shall guide them:
but the perverseness of transgressors shall
destroy them.

~PROVERBS 11:3

~~~~~~~~~~~~~~~~~~~~~~~~~~

Recompense
to no man
evil for evil.
Provide
things honest
in the sight
of all men.

~ROMANS 12:17

LIE not one to another, seeing that ye have put off the old man with his deeds.

~*COLOSSIANS 3:9*

~~~~~~~~~~~~~~~~~~~~~~~~

THOU shalt not bear false witness against thy neighbor.

~*EXODUS 20:16*

~~~~~~~~~~~~~~~~~~~~~~~~

Hope

FOR we are saved by hope: but hope that is seen is not hope: for what a man seeth, why doth he yet hope for? But if we hope for that we see not, then do we with patience wait for it.

~ROMANS 8:24–25

FOR with God nothing shall be impossible.

~LUKE 1:37

BE of good courage, and he shall strengthen your heart, all ye that hope in the LORD.

~PSALMS 31:24

FOR there is hope of a tree, if it be cut down, that it will sprout again, and that the tender branch thereof will not cease.

~JOB 14:7

AND now, Lord, what wait I for? My hope is in thee.

~PSALMS 39:7

BLESSED is the man that trusteth in the
LORD, and whose hope the LORD is.

~JEREMIAH 17:7

THE LORD shall preserve thee from all evil:
he shall preserve thy soul.

~PSALMS 121:7

HOPE deferred maketh the heart sick: but
when the desire cometh, it is a tree of life.

~PROVERBS 13:12

Why art thou cast
down, O my soul?
and why art thou
disquieted within me?
hope thou in God:
for I shall yet praise
him, who is the health
of my countenance,
and my God.

~PSALMS 42:11

Humility

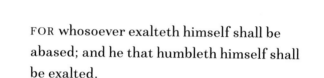

FOR whosoever exalteth himself shall be abased; and he that humbleth himself shall be exalted.

~LUKE 14:11

...VANITY of vanities; all is vanity.

~ECCLESIASTES 1:2

WHEN men are cast down, then thou shalt say, There is lifting up; and he shall save the humble person.

~JOB 22:29

HUMBLE yourselves in the sight of the Lord, and he shall lift you up.

~JAMES 4:10

...GOD resisteth the proud, and giveth grace to the humble.

~1 PETER 5:5

IF we say that we have no sin, we deceive ourselves, and the truth is not in us.

~1 JOHN 1:8

PRIDE goeth before destruction, and an haughty spirit before a fall. Better it is to be of an humble spirit with the lowly, than to divide the spoil with the proud.

~PROVERBS 16:18–19

BY humility and the fear of the LORD are riches, and honour, and life.

~PROVERBS 22:4

JUDGE not, that ye be not judged.

~MATTHEW 7:1

IF my people, which are called by my name, shall humble themselves, and pray, and seek my face, and turn from their wicked ways; then will I hear from heaven, and will forgive their sin, and will heal their land.

~2 CHRONICLES 7:14

DO ye think that the scripture saith in vain, The spirit that dwelleth in us lusteth to envy? But he giveth more grace. Wherefore he saith, God resisteth the proud, but giveth grace unto the humble.

~JAMES 4:5–6

BUT so shall it not be among you: but whosoever will be great among you, shall be your minister: And whosoever of you will be the chiefest, shall be servant of all. For even the Son of man came not to be ministered unto, but to minister, and to give his life a ransom for many.

~MARK 10:43–45

THE fear of the LORD is the instruction of wisdom; and before honour is humility.

~PROVERBS 15:33

Inspiration

HE only is my rock and my salvation: he is my defence; I shall not be moved.

~PSALMS 62:6

BE strong and of a good courage, fear not, nor be afraid of them: for the LORD thy God, he it is that doth go with thee; he will not fail thee, nor forsake thee.

~DEUTERONOMY 31:6

FOR the Holy Ghost shall teach you in the same hour what ye ought to say.

~LUKE 12:12

BUT my God shall supply all your need according to his riches in glory by Christ Jesus.

~PHILIPPIANS 4:19

FOR our light affliction, which is but for a moment, worketh for us a far more exceeding and eternal weight of glory.

~2 CORINTHIANS 4:17

BUT Jesus beheld them, and said unto them, With men this is impossible; but with God all things are possible.

~MATTHEW 19:26

FOR I the LORD thy God will hold thy right hand, saying unto thee, Fear not; I will help thee.

~ISAIAH 41:13

WHEN thou passest through the waters, I will be with thee; and through the rivers, they shall not overflow thee: when thou walkest through the fire, thou shalt not be burned; neither shall the flame kindle upon thee.

~ISAIAH 43:2

IN my distress I cried unto the LORD, and he heard me.

~PSALMS 120:1

FOR I am persuaded, that neither death, nor life, nor angels, nor principalities, nor powers, nor things present, nor things to come, nor height, nor depth, nor any other creature, shall be able to separate us from the love of God, which is in Christ Jesus our Lord.

~ROMANS 8:38–39

Integrity

BE not overcome of evil, but overcome evil
with good.

~ROMANS 12:21

HAVING a good conscience; that, whereas
they speak evil of you, as of evildoers, they
may be ashamed that falsely accuse your
good conversation in Christ.

~1 PETER 3:16

TO do justice and judgment is more
acceptable to the LORD than sacrifice.

~PROVERBS 21:3

LET integrity and uprightness preserve me;
for I wait on thee.

~PSALMS 25:21

MY righteousness I hold fast, and will not let
it go: my heart shall not reproach me so long
as I live.

~JOB 27:6

PRAY for us: for we trust we have a good
conscience, in all things willing to live honestly.

~HEBREWS 13:18

IN all things shewing thyself a pattern of good
works: in doctrine shewing uncorruptness,
gravity, sincerity.

~TITUS 2:7

THAT we henceforth be no more children, tossed to and fro, and carried about with every wind of doctrine, by the sleight of men, and cunning craftiness, whereby they lie in wait to deceive.

~*EPHESIANS 4:14*

THE way of the just is uprightness: thou, most upright, dost weigh the path of the just.

~*ISAIAH 26:7*

DEPART from evil, and do good; and dwell for evermore.

~*PSALMS 37:27*

Jealousy

WRATH is cruel, and anger is outrageous; but who is able to stand before envy?

~PSALMS 27:4

FOR where envying and strife is, there is confusion and every evil work.

~JAMES 3:16

IF we live in the Spirit, let us also walk in the Spirit. Let us not be desirous of vain glory, provoking one another, envying one another.

~GALATIANS 5:25–26

BE not thou envious against evil men, neither desire to be with them.

~*PROVERBS 24:1*

FOR I was envious at the foolish, when I saw the prosperity of the wicked.

~*PSALMS 73:3*

A sound heart is the life of the flesh: but envy the rottenness of the bones.

~*PROVERBS 14:30*

FOR he knew that the chief priests had delivered him for envy.

~*MARK 15:10*

Ye lust, and have
not: ye kill, and
desire to have, and
cannot obtain:
ye fight and war,
yet ye have not,
because ye ask not.

~JAMES 4:2

Joy
AND CELEBRATION

WHOM having not seen, ye love; in whom,
though now ye see him not, yet believing, ye
rejoice with joy unspeakable and full of glory.

~1 PETER 1:8

THE joy of the Lord is your strength.

~NEHEMIAH 8:10

AND thou shalt have joy and gladness; and
many shall rejoice at his birth.

~LUKE 1:14

THOU hast turned for me my mourning into dancing: thou hast put off my sackcloth, and girded me with gladness.

~PSALMS 30:11

THEN the people rejoiced, for that they offered willingly, because with perfect heart they offered willingly to the LORD.

~1 CHRONICLES 29:9

THESE things have I spoken unto you, that my joy might remain in you, and that your joy might be full.

~JOHN 15:11

O clap your hands, all ye people; shout unto God with the voice of triumph.

~PSALMS 47:1

IT is a good thing to give thanks unto the Lord, and to sing praises unto thy name, O most High.

~*PSALMS 92:1*

PRAISE ye the LORD. Praise God in his sanctuary: praise him in the firmament of his power. Praise him for his mighty acts: praise him according to his excellent greatness. Praise him with the sound of the trumpet: praise him with the psaltery and harp. Praise him with the timbrel and dance: praise him with stringed instruments and organs. Praise him upon the loud cymbals: praise him upon the high sounding cymbals.

~*PSALMS 150:1–5*

REJOICE in the Lord alway: and again I say, Rejoice.

~*PHILIPPIANS 4:4*

Knowledge
AND WISDOM

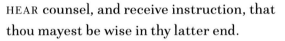

HEAR counsel, and receive instruction, that thou mayest be wise in thy latter end.

~PROVERBS 19:20

MY people are destroyed for lack of knowledge.

~HOSEA 4:6

THE heart of the prudent getteth knowledge; and the ear of the wise seeketh knowledge.

~PROVERBS 18:15

PROFESSING themselves to be wise, they became fools.

~ROMANS 1:22

BEHOLD, I send you forth as sheep in the midst of wolves: be ye therefore wise as serpents, and harmless as doves.

~MATTHEW 10:16

HEAR instruction, and be wise, and refuse it not.

~PROVERBS 8:33

THEREFORE is judgment far from us, neither doth justice overtake us: we wait for light, but behold obscurity; for brightness, but we walk in darkness.

~ISAIAH 59:9

WHEN wisdom entereth into thine heart, and knowledge is pleasant unto thy soul; Discretion shall preserve thee, understanding shall keep thee.

~*PROVERBS 2:10–11*

THOU hast dealt well with thy servant, O LORD, according unto thy word. Teach me good judgment and knowledge: for I have believed thy commandments.

~*PSALMS 119:65–66*

AND they that be wise shall shine as the brightness of the firmament; and they that turn many to righteousness as the stars for ever and ever.

~*DANIEL 12:13*

Love

LET him kiss me with the kisses of his mouth:
for thy love is better than wine.

~SONG OF SOLOMON 1:2

BELOVED, let us love one another: for love is
of God; and every one that loveth is born of
God, and knoweth God.

~1 JOHN 4:7

THIS is my commandment, That ye love one
another, as I have loved you.

~JOHN 15:12

HATRED stirreth up strifes: but love
covereth all sins.

~*PROVERBS 10:12*

THERE is no fear in love; but perfect love
casteth out fear: because fear hath torment.

~*1 JOHN 4:18*

LET love be without dissimulation.
Abhor that which is evil; cleave to that
which is good.

~*ROMANS 12:9*

AS the Father hath loved me, so have I loved
you: continue ye in my love.

~*JOHN 15:9*

YE have heard that it hath been said, Thou shalt love thy neighbour, and hate thine enemy. But I say unto you, Love your enemies, bless them that curse you, do good to them that hate you, and pray for them which despitefully use you, and persecute you.

~MATTHEW 5:43–44

SET me as a seal upon thine heart, as a seal upon thine arm: for love is strong as death; jealousy is cruel as the grave: the coals thereof are coals of fire, which hath a most vehement flame. Many waters cannot quench love, neither can the floods drown it.

~SONG OF SOLOMON 8:6–7

Charity suffereth
long, and is kind;
charity envieth
not; charity
vaunteth not itself,
is not puffed up.

~1 CORINTHIANS 13:4

Marriage
AND RELATIONSHIPS

MY beloved is mine, and I am his.

~SONG OF SOLOMON 2:16

WHAT therefore God hath joined together, let not man put asunder.

~MARK 10:9

HOUSE and riches are the inheritance of fathers: and a prudent wife is from the LORD.

~PROVERBS 19:14

WITH all lowliness and meekness, with longsuffering, forbearing one another in love.

~EPHESIANS 4:2

~~~~~~~~~~~~~~~~~~~~~~~~~~~~

BETTER is a dry morsel, and quietness therewith, than an house full of sacrifices with strife.

~PROVERBS 17:1

~~~~~~~~~~~~~~~~~~~~~~~~~~~~

A new commandment I give unto you, That ye love one another; as I have loved you, that ye also love one another.

~JOHN 13:34

BELOVED, if God so loved us, we ought also to love one another.

~1 JOHN 4:11

TWO are better than one; because they have a good reward for their labour.

~ECCLESIASTES 4:9

...WALK in love, as Christ also hath loved us.

~EPHESIANS 5:2

WHOSO findeth a wife findeth a good thing, and obtaineth favour of the LORD.

~PROVERBS 18:22

Mercy

BE ye therefore merciful, as your Father also is merciful.

~LUKE 6:36

FOR as the heaven is high above the earth, so great is his mercy toward them that fear him.

~PSALMS 103:11

LET all bitterness, and wrath, and anger, and clamour, and evil speaking, be put away from you, with all malice.

~EPHESIANS 4:31

BE merciful unto me, O Lord: for I cry unto thee daily.

~PSALMS 86:3

BLESSED are the merciful: for they shall obtain mercy.

~MATTHEW 5:7

AND rend your heart, and not your garments, and turn unto the LORD your God: for he is gracious and merciful, slow to anger, and of great kindness, and repenteth him of the evil.

~JOEL 2:13

WITHHOLD not thou thy tender mercies from me, O LORD: let thy lovingkindness and thy truth continually preserve me.

~PSALMS 40:11

WHO is a God like unto thee, that pardoneth iniquity, and passeth by the transgression of the remnant of his heritage? he retaineth not his anger for ever, because he delighteth in mercy.

~MICAH 7:18

BUT God, who is rich in mercy, for his great love wherewith he loved us, Even when we were dead in sins, hath quickened us together with Christ, (by grace ye are saved;) And hath raised us up together, and made us sit together in heavenly places in Christ Jesus.

~EPHESIANS 2:4–6

HE hath shewed thee, O man, what is good; and what doth the LORD require of thee, but to do justly, and to love mercy, and to walk humbly with thy God?

~MICAH 6:8

Miracles

THEN those men, when they had seen the miracle that Jesus did, said, This is of a truth that prophet that should come into the world.

~JOHN 6:14

HE is thy praise, and he is thy God, that hath done for thee these great and terrible things, which thine eyes have seen.

~DEUTERONOMY 10:21

JESUS said unto him, If thou canst believe, all things are possible to him that believeth.

~MARK 9:23

I would seek unto God, and unto God would I commit my cause: Which doeth great things and unsearchable; marvellous things without number: Who giveth rain upon the earth, and sendeth waters upon the fields: To set up on high those that be low; that those which mourn may be exalted to safety.

~JOB 5:8–11

AND his name through faith in his name hath made this man strong, whom ye see and know: yea, the faith which is by him hath given him this perfect soundness in the presence of you all.

~ACTS 3:16

THROUGH mighty signs and wonders, by the power of the Spirit of God; so that from Jerusalem, and round about unto Illyricum, I have fully preached the gospel of Christ.

~ROMANS 15:19

AND now, Lord, behold their threatenings: and grant unto thy servants, that with all boldness they may speak thy word, By stretching forth thine hand to heal; and that signs and wonders may be done by the name of thy holy child Jesus. And when they had prayed, the place was shaken where they were assembled together; and they were all filled with the Holy Ghost, and they spake the word of God with boldness.

~ACTS 4:29–31

THEN said Jesus unto him, Except ye see signs and wonders, ye will not believe.

~JOHN 4:48

BEHOLD, I am the LORD, the God of all flesh: is there any thing too hard for me?

~JEREMIAH 32:27

And these signs
shall follow them
that believe; In my
name shall they
cast out devils;
they shall speak
with new tongues.

~MARK 16:17

Moderation
AND SELF-CONTROL

LET your moderation be known unto all men.
The Lord is at hand.

~PHILIPPIANS 4:5

HAST thou found honey? eat so much as
is sufficient for thee, lest thou be filled
therewith, and vomit it.

~PROVERBS 25:16

MEEKNESS, temperance: against such there
is no law.

~GALATIANS 5:23

WHAT? know ye not that your body is the
temple of the Holy Ghost which is in you, which
ye have of God, and ye are not your own?

~*1 CORINTHIANS 6:19*

TEACHING us that, denying ungodliness
and worldly lusts, we should live soberly,
righteously, and godly, in this present world.

~*TITUS 2:12*

THEREFORE let us not sleep, as do others; but
let us watch and be sober.

~*1 THESSALONIANS 5:6*

WATCH and pray, that ye enter not into
temptation: the spirit indeed is willing, but
the flesh is weak.

~*MATTHEW 26:41*

Look to
yourselves, that
we lose not those
things which we
have wrought, but
that we receive a
full reward.

~2 JOHN 1:8

FOR if ye live after the flesh, ye shall die: but if ye through the Spirit do mortify the deeds of the body, ye shall live.

~*ROMANS 8:13*

BUT I keep under my body, and bring it into subjection: lest that by any means, when I have preached to others, I myself should be a castaway.

~*1 CORINTHIANS 9:27*

Motherhood

WHO can find a virtuous woman? for her price is far above rubies.

~PROVERBS 31:10

I would lead thee, and bring thee into my mother's house, who would instruct me: I would cause thee to drink of spiced wine of the juice of my pomegranate.

~SONG OF SOLOMON 8:2

HER children arise up, and call her blessed; her husband also, and he praiseth her.

~PROVERBS 31:28

NOW there stood by the cross of Jesus his mother, and his mother's sister, Mary the wife of Cleophas, and Mary Magdalene. When Jesus therefore saw his mother, and the disciple standing by, whom he loved, he saith unto his mother, Woman, behold thy son! Then saith he to the disciple, Behold thy mother! And from that hour that disciple took her unto his own home.

~JOHN 19:26–27

THAT they may teach the young women to be sober, to love their husbands, to love their children.

~TITUS 2:4

AS one whom his mother comforteth, so will I comfort you; and ye shall be comforted in Jerusalem.

~ISAIAH 66:13

SHE looketh well to the ways of her household, and eateth not the bread of idleness.

~PROVERBS 31:27

AND he went down with them, and came to Nazareth, and was subject unto them: but his mother kept all these sayings in her heart.

~LUKE 2:51

HE hath made every thing beautiful in his time: also he hath set the world in their heart, so that no man can find out the work that God maketh from the beginning to the end.

~ECCLESIASTES 3:11

YEA, the darkness hideth not from thee; but the night shineth as the day: the darkness and the light are both alike to thee. For thou hast possessed my reins: thou hast covered me in my mother's womb.

~PSALMS 139:12–13

A woman when she is in travail hath sorrow, because her hour is come: but as soon as she is delivered of the child, she remembereth no more the anguish, for joy that a man is born into the world.

~JOHN 16:21

Nature's
WONDERS

OUT of Zion, the perfection of beauty, God
hath shined.

~PSALMS 50:2

ALL things were made by him; and without
him was not any thing made that was made.

~JOHN 1:3

THE heavens declare the glory of God; and
the firmament sheweth his handywork.

~PSALMS 19:1

IN his hand are the deep places of the earth: the strength of the hills is his also. The sea is his, and he made it: and his hands formed the dry land.

~PSALMS 95:4–5

HE sendeth the springs into the valleys, which run among the hills. They give drink to every beast of the field: the wild asses quench their thirst. By them shall the fowls of the heaven have their habitation, which sing among the branches.

~PSALMS 104:10–12

O LORD, how manifold are thy works! in wisdom hast thou made them all: the earth is full of thy riches.

~PSALMS 104:24

THIS is the LORD's doing; it is marvellous in our eyes.

~*PSALMS 118:23*

FOR the invisible things of him from the creation of the world are clearly seen, being understood by the things that are made, even his eternal power and Godhead; so that they are without excuse.

~*ROMANS 1:20*

REMEMBER ye not the former things, neither consider the things of old. Behold, I will do a new thing; now it shall spring forth; shall ye not know it? I will even make a way in the wilderness, and rivers in the desert. The beast of the field shall honour me, the dragons and the owls: because I give waters in the wilderness, and rivers in the desert, to give drink to my people, my chosen.

~*ISAIAH 43:18–20*

CONSIDER the lilies how they grow: they toil
not, they spin not; and yet I say unto you,
that Solomon in all his glory was not arrayed
like one of these.

~LUKE 12:27

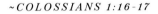

FOR by him were all things created, that
are in heaven, and that are in earth, visible
and invisible, whether they be thrones, or
dominions, or principalities, or powers: all
things were created by him, and for him:
and he is before all things, and by him all
things consist.

~COLOSSIANS 1:16-17

Patience

BE not hasty in thy spirit to be angry: for anger resteth in the bosom of fools.

~ECCLESIASTES 7:9

BUT let patience have her perfect work, that ye may be perfect and entire, wanting nothing.

~JAMES 1:4

FOR ye have need of patience, that, after ye have done the will of God, ye might receive the promise.

~HEBREWS 10:36

BE ye also patient; stablish your hearts: for the coming of the Lord draweth nigh.

~JAMES 5:8

BE not rash with thy mouth.

~ECCLESIASTES 5:2

I waited patiently for the LORD; and he inclined unto me, and heard my cry.

~PSALMS 40:1

WHEREFORE seeing we also are compassed about with so great a cloud of witnesses, let us lay aside every weight, and the sin which doth so easily beset us, and let us run with patience the race that is set before us.

~ROMANS 12:1

REST in the LORD, and wait patiently for him: fret not thyself because of him who prospereth in his way, because of the man who bringeth wicked devices to pass.

~PSALMS 37:7

BECAUSE thou hast kept the word of my patience, I also will keep thee from the hour of temptation, which shall come upon all the world, to try them that dwell upon the earth.

~REVELATIONS 3:10

AND we desire that every one of you do shew the same diligence to the full assurance of hope unto the end: That ye be not slothful, but followers of them who through faith and patience inherit the promises.

~HEBREWS 6:11–12

But the fruit
of the Spirit is
love, joy, peace,
longsuffering,
gentleness,
goodness, faith.

~JAMES 5:22

Peace

BLESSED are the peacemakers: for they shall be called the children of God.

~MATTHEW 5:9

NOW the Lord of peace himself give you peace always by all means. The Lord be with you all.

~2 THESSALONIANS 3:16

THEREFORE being justified by faith, we have peace with God through our Lord Jesus Christ.

~ROMANS 5:1

IF it be possible, as much as lieth in you, live peaceably with all men.

~ROMANS 12:18

PEACE I leave with you, my peace I give unto you: not as the world giveth, give I unto you. Let not your heart be troubled, neither let it be afraid.

~JOHN 14:27

HE hath delivered my soul in peace from the battle that was against me: for there were many with me.

~PSALMS 55:18

FULFIL ye my joy, that ye be likeminded, having the same love, being of one accord, of one mind.

~PHILIPPIANS 2:2

LET us therefore follow after the things which make for peace, and things wherewith one may edify another.

~ROMANS 14:19

FOR if, when we were enemies, we were reconciled to God by the death of his Son, much more, being reconciled, we shall be saved by his life.

~ROMANS 5:10

FOR the mountains shall depart, and the hills be removed; but my kindness shall not depart from thee, neither shall the covenant of my peace be removed, saith the LORD that hath mercy on thee.

~ISAIAH 54:10

BETTER is an handful with quietness, than both the hands full with travail and vexation of spirit.

~*ECCLESIASTES 4:6*

I will hear what God the LORD will speak: for he will speak peace unto his people, and to his saints: but let them not turn again to folly. Surely his salvation is nigh them that fear him; that glory may dwell in our land. Mercy and truth are met together; righteousness and peace have kissed each other.

~*PSALMS 85:8–10*

ONLY let your conversation be as it becometh the gospel of Christ: that whether I come and see you, or else be absent, I may hear of your affairs, that ye stand fast in one spirit, with one mind striving together for the faith of the gospel.

~*PHILIPPIANS 1:27*

Perseverance

AND not only so, but we glory in tribulations also: knowing that tribulation worketh patience; And patience, experience; and experience, hope.

~ROMANS 5:3–4

BUT he that shall endure unto the end, the same shall be saved.

~MATTHEW 24:13

THOU therefore endure hardness, as a good soldier of Jesus Christ.

~2 TIMOTHY 2:3

BEHOLD, we count them happy which endure. Ye have heard of the patience of Job, and have seen the end of the Lord; that the Lord is very pitiful, and of tender mercy.

~JAMES 5:11

IF thou shalt do this thing, and God command thee so, then thou shalt be able to endure, and all this people shall also go to their place in peace.

~EXODUS 18:23

But they that wait
upon the LORD
shall renew their
strength; they shall
mount up with wings
as eagles; they shall
run, and not be
weary; and they shall
walk, and not faint.

~ISAIAH 40:31

FOR I reckon that the sufferings of this present time are not worthy to be compared with the glory which shall be revealed in us.

~ROMANS 8:18

SO that we ourselves glory in you in the churches of God for your patience and faith in all your persecutions and tribulations that ye endure.

~2 THESSALONIANS 1:4

KNOW ye not that they which run in a race run all, but one receiveth the prize? So run, that ye may obtain.

~1 CORINTHIANS 9:24

TO them who by patient continuance in well doing seek for glory and honour and immortality, eternal life.

~ROMANS 2:7

Prayer

CALL unto me, and I will answer thee, and shew thee great and mighty things, which thou knowest not.

~JEREMIAH 33:3

I waited patiently for the LORD; and he inclined unto me, and heard my cry. He brought me up also out of an horrible pit, out of the miry clay, and set my feet upon a rock, and established my goings. And he hath put a new song in my mouth, even praise unto our God: many shall see it, and fear, and shall trust in the LORD.

~PSALMS 40:1–3

HEAR the right, O LORD, attend unto my cry, give ear unto my prayer, that goeth not out of feigned lips. Let my sentence come forth from thy presence; let thine eyes behold the things that are equal. Thou hast proved mine heart; thou hast visited me in the night; thou hast tried me, and shalt find nothing; I am purposed that my mouth shall not transgress.

~PSALMS 17:1–3

HEAR, O LORD, when I cry with my voice: have mercy also upon me, and answer me. When thou saidst, Seek ye my face; my heart said unto thee, Thy face, LORD, will I seek. Hide not thy face far from me; put not thy servant away in anger: thou hast been my help; leave me not, neither forsake me, O God of my salvation.

~PSALMS 27:7–9

AND I say unto you, Ask, and it shall be given you; seek, and ye shall find; knock, and it shall be opened unto you.

~LUKE 11:9

GIVE ear, O LORD, unto my prayer; and attend to the voice of my supplications. In the day of my trouble I will call upon thee: for thou wilt answer me.

~PSALMS 86:6–7

MY heart is fixed, O God, my heart is fixed: I will sing and give praise.

~PSALMS 57:7

OUT of the depths have I cried unto thee, O LORD. Lord, hear my voice: let thine ears be attentive to the voice of my supplications.

~PSALMS 130:1–2

LET my prayer be set forth before thee as incense; and the lifting up of my hands as the evening sacrifice.

~PSALMS 141:2

BUT thou, when thou prayest, enter into thy closet, and when thou hast shut thy door, pray to thy Father which is in secret; and thy Father which seeth in secret shall reward thee openly. But when ye pray, use not vain repetitions, as the heathen do: for they think that they shall be heard for their much speaking.

~MATTHEW 6:6–7

AND this is the confidence that we have in him, that, if we ask any thing according to his will, he heareth us.

~1 JOHN 5:14

Preaching

AND TEACHING

AND he said unto them, Go ye into all the world, and preach the gospel to every creature.

~MARK 16:15

FOR many are called, but few are chosen.

~MATTHEW 22:14

...THE Lord ordained that they which preach the gospel should live of the gospel.

~1 CORINTHIANS 9:14

GOOD and upright is the LORD: therefore
will he teach sinners in the way. The meek
will he guide in judgment: and the meek will
he teach his way.

~*PSALMS 25:8-9*

TEACH me to do thy will; for thou art my God:
thy spirit is good; lead me into the land of
uprightness.

~*PSALMS 143:10*

PREACH the word; be instant in season, out of season; reprove, rebuke, exhort with all longsuffering and doctrine.

~2 TIMOTHY 4:2

I will instruct thee and teach thee in the way which thou shalt go: I will guide thee with mine eye.

~PSALMS 32:8

TEACH me thy way, O LORD; I will walk in thy truth: unite my heart to fear thy name. I will praise thee, O Lord my God, with all my heart: and I will glorify thy name for evermore.

~PSALMS 86:11-12

JESUS answered them, and said, My doctrine is not mine, but his that sent me.

~JOHN 7:16

AND daily in the temple, and in every house, they ceased not to teach and preach Jesus Christ.

~ACTS 5:42

THE Spirit of the Lord GOD is upon me; because the LORD hath anointed me to preach good tidings unto the meek; he hath sent me to bind up the brokenhearted, to proclaim liberty to the captives, and the opening of the prison to them that are bound.

~ISAIAH 61:1

AND I saw another angel fly in the midst of heaven, having the everlasting gospel to preach unto them that dwell on the earth, and to every nation, and kindred, and tongue, and people.

~REVELATIONS 14:6

Presence

OF GOD

AND they heard the voice of the LORD God walking in the garden in the cool of the day: and Adam and his wife hid themselves from the presence of the LORD God amongst the trees of the garden.

~GENESIS 3:8

FOR we are strangers before thee, and sojourners, as were all our fathers: our days on the earth are as a shadow, and there is none abiding.

~1 CHRONICLES 29:15

GOD be merciful unto us, and bless us; and cause his face to shine upon us.

~PSALMS 67:1

BLESSED is the people that know the joyful sound: they shall walk, O LORD, in the light of thy countenance. In thy name shall they rejoice all the day: and in thy righteousness shall they be exalted.

~PSALMS 89:16

I am with you alway, even unto the end of the world. Amen.

~MATTHEW 28:20

FOR where two or three are gathered together in my name, there am I in the midst of them.

~MATTHEW 18:20

BEHOLD, the hour cometh, yea, is now come, that ye shall be scattered, every man to his own, and shall leave me alone: and yet I am not alone, because the Father is with me.

~JOHN 16:32

FOR mine eyes are upon all their ways: they are not hid from my face, neither is their iniquity hid from mine eyes.

~JEREMIAH 16:17

THOU wilt shew me the path of life: in thy presence is fulness of joy; at thy right hand there are pleasures for evermore.

~PSALMS 16:11

... I foresaw the Lord always before my face, for he is on my right hand, that I should not be moved.

~ACTS 2:25

AND, behold, I am with thee, and will keep thee in all places whither thou goest, and will bring thee again into this land; for I will not leave thee, until I have done that which I have spoken to thee of.

~GENESIS 28:15

~~~~~~

FOR as the lightning, that lighteneth out of the one part under heaven, shineth unto the other part under heaven; so shall also the Son of man be in his day.

~LUKE 17:24

~~~~~~

Prudence

A fool's wrath is presently known: but a prudent man covereth shame.

~PROVERBS 12:16

A fool despiseth his father's instruction: but he that regardeth reproof is prudent.

~PROVERBS 15:5

A prudent man foreseeth the evil, and hideth himself; but the simple pass on, and are punished.

~PROVERBS 27:12

THE simple believeth every word: but the prudent man looketh well to his going. A wise man feareth, and departeth from evil: but the fool rageth, and is confident.

~PROVERBS 14:15–16

WOE unto them that are wise in their own eyes, and prudent in their own sight!

~ISAIAH 5:21

PROVE all things; hold fast that which is good.

~1 THESSALONIANS 5:21

THEREFORE the prudent shall keep silence in that time; for it is an evil time.

~AMOS 5:13

RECEIVE my instruction, and not silver; and knowledge rather than choice gold. For wisdom is better than rubies; and all the things that may be desired are not to be compared to it. I wisdom dwell with prudence, and find out knowledge of witty inventions.

~PROVERBS 8:10–12

Wisdom is good
with an inheritance:
and by it there is profit
to them that see the sun.
For wisdom is a defence,
and money is a defence:
but the excellency of
knowledge is, that
wisdom giveth life to
them that have it.

~ECCLESIASTES 7:11–12

Salvation

BUT the meek shall inherit the earth;
and shall delight themselves in the
abundance of peace.

~PSALMS 37:11

THE LORD is my strength and song, and is
become my salvation.

~PSALMS 118:14

AND it shall come to pass, that whosoever
shall call on the name of the Lord
shall be saved.

~ACTS 2:21

FOR whatsoever is born of God overcometh the world: and this is the victory that overcometh the world, even our faith.

~1 JOHN 5:4

BUT God will redeem my soul from the power of the grave: for he shall receive me.

~PSALMS 49:15

I have gone astray like a lost sheep;
seek thy servant; for I do not forget thy commandments.

~PSALMS 119:176

BEHOLD, God is my salvation; I will trust, and not be afraid: for the LORD JEHOVAH is my strength and my song; he also is become my salvation.

~ISAIAH 12:2

FOR even hereunto were ye called: because Christ also suffered for us, leaving us an example, that ye should follow his steps. Who did no sin, neither was guile found in his mouth: Who, when he was reviled, reviled not again; when he suffered, he threatened not; but committed himself to him that judgeth righteously: Who his own self bare our sins in his own body on the tree, that we, being dead to sins, should live unto righteousness: by whose stripes ye were healed.

~1 PETER 2:21–24

I have fought a good fight, I have finished my course, I have kept the faith: Henceforth there is laid up for me a crown of righteousness, which the Lord, the righteous judge, shall give me at that day: and not to me only, but unto all them also that love his appearing.

~2 TIMOTHY 4:7–8

NOW if we be dead with Christ, we believe that we shall also live with him: Knowing that Christ being raised from the dead dieth no more; death hath no more dominion over him.

~ROMANS 6:8–9

EVERY valley shall be filled, and every mountain and hill shall be brought low; and the crooked shall be made straight, and the rough ways shall be made smooth; And all flesh shall see the salvation of God.

~LUKE 3:5–6

Seeking
FORGIVENESS

REMEMBER, I pray thee, who ever perished,
being innocent? or where were the
righteous cut off?

~JOB 4:7

ALL we like sheep have gone astray...

~ISAIAH 53:6

IF we confess our sins, he is faithful and just
to forgive us our sins, and to cleanse us from
all unrighteousness.

~1 JOHN 1:9

I, even I, am he that blotteth out thy transgressions for mine own sake, and will not remember thy sins.

~ISAIAH 43:25

THAT if thou shalt confess with thy mouth the Lord Jesus, and shalt believe in thine heart that God hath raised him from the dead, thou shalt be saved.

~ROMANS 10:9

THEN said Jesus to them again, Peace be unto you: as my Father hath sent me, even so send I you. And when he had said this, he breathed on them, and saith unto them, Receive ye the Holy Ghost: Whose soever sins ye remit, they are remitted unto them; and whose soever sins ye retain, they are retained.

~JOHN 20:21–23

I acknowledge my sin unto thee, and mine iniquity have I not hid. I said, I will confess my transgressions unto the LORD; and thou forgavest the iniquity of my sin.

~PSALMS 32:5

REPENT ye therefore, and be converted, that your sins may be blotted out, when the times of refreshing shall come from the presence of the Lord.

~ACTS 3:19

I came not to call the righteous, but sinners to repentance.

~LUKE 5:32

CONFESS your faults one to another, and pray one for another, that ye may be healed.

~JAMES 5:16

THEN Peter said unto them, Repent, and be baptized every one of you in the name of Jesus Christ for the remission of sins, and ye shall receive the gift of the Holy Ghost.

~ACTS 2:38

FOR whosoever shall call upon the name of the Lord shall be saved.

~ROMANS 10:13

HE that covereth his sins shall not prosper: but whoso confesseth and forsaketh them shall have mercy.

~PSALMS 28:13

Serenity

SIX days thou shalt work, but on the seventh day thou shalt rest: in earing time and in harvest thou shalt rest.

~EXODUS 34:21

AND I said, Oh that I had wings like a dove! for then would I fly away, and be at rest.

~PSALMS 55:6

SURELY goodness and mercy shall follow me all the days of my life: and I will dwell in the house of the LORD for ever.

~PSALMS 23:6

RETURN unto thy rest, O my soul; for the LORD hath dealt bountifully with thee. For thou hast delivered my soul from death, mine eyes from tears, and my feet from falling.

~PSALMS 116:7–8

THERE be many that say, Who will shew us any good? LORD, lift thou up the light of thy countenance upon us. Thou hast put gladness in my heart, more than in the time that their corn and their wine increased. I will both lay me down in peace, and sleep: for thou, LORD, only makest me dwell in safety.

~ROMANS 4:6–8

CAST thy burden upon the LORD, and he shall sustain thee: he shall never suffer the righteous to be moved.

~PSALMS 55:22

...FOR I have learned, in whatsoever state I am, therewith to be content.

~PHILIPPIANS 4:11

MERCY unto you, and peace, and love, be multiplied.

~JUDE 1:2

NAKED came I out of my mother's womb, and naked shall I return thither: the LORD gave, and the LORD hath taken away; blessed be the name of the LORD...

~JOB 1:21

THOU wilt keep him in perfect peace, whose mind is stayed on thee: because he trusteth in thee.

~ISAIAH 26:3

FOR our light affliction, which is but for a moment, worketh for us a far more exceeding and eternal weight of glory; While we look not at the things which are seen, but at the things which are not seen: for the things which are seen are temporal; but the things which are not seen are eternal.

~*2 PAUL 4:17–18*

Serving

THOU shalt fear the LORD thy God, and serve him, and shalt swear by his name.

~DEUTERONOMY 6:13

SEE, I have set before thee this day life and good, and death and evil; In that I command thee this day to love the LORD thy God, to walk in his ways, and to keep his commandments and his statutes and his judgments, that thou mayest live and multiply: and the LORD thy God shall bless thee in the land whither thou goest to possess it.

~DEUTERONOMY 30:15–16

BUT take diligent heed to do the commandment and the law, which Moses the servant of the LORD charged you, to love the LORD your God, and to walk in all his ways, and to keep his commandments, and to cleave unto him, and to serve him with all your heart and with all your soul.

~JOSHUA 22:5

FOR God is not unrighteous to forget your work and labour of love, which ye have shewed toward his name, in that ye have ministered to the saints, and do minister.

~HEBREWS 6:10

BUT to do good and to communicate forget not: for with such sacrifices God is well pleased.

~HEBREWS 13:16

For the poor shall
never cease out of
the land: therefore
I command thee,
saying, Thou shalt
open thine hand
wide unto thy
brother, to thy poor,
and to thy needy,
in thy land.

~DEUTERONOMY 15:11

FOR we are his workmanship, created
in Christ Jesus unto good works, which
God hath before ordained that we should
walk in them.

~EPHESIANS 2:10

ONLY fear the LORD, and serve him in truth
with all your heart: for consider how great
things he hath done for you.

~1 SAMUEL 12:24

BE ye strong therefore, and let not your hands
be weak: for your work shall be rewarded.

~2 CHRONICLES 15:7

Stewardship

THE heaven, even the heavens, are the LORD's: but the earth hath he given to the children of men.

~PSALMS 115:16

THE earth is the LORD's, and the fulness thereof; the world, and they that dwell therein.

~PSALMS 24:1

THE land shall not be sold for ever: for the land is mine, for ye are strangers and sojourners with me.

~LEVITICUS 25:23

AND God said, Let us make man in our image, after our likeness: and let them have dominion over the fish of the sea, and over the fowl of the air, and over the cattle, and over all the earth, and over every creeping thing that creepeth upon the earth.

~GENESIS 1:26

THEY shall not hurt nor destroy in all my holy mountain: for the earth shall be full of the knowledge of the LORD, as the waters cover the sea.

~ISAIAH 11:9

SO ye shall not pollute the land wherein ye are: for blood it defileth the land: and the land cannot be cleansed of the blood that is shed therein, but by the blood of him that shed it.

~NUMBERS 35:33

FOR a bishop must be blameless, as the steward of God; not selfwilled, not soon angry, not given to wine, no striker, not given to filthy lucre.

~ TITUS 1:7

I the LORD do keep it; I will water it every moment: lest any hurt it, I will keep it night and day.

~ISAIAH 27:3

SEEMETH it a small thing unto you to have eaten up the good pasture, but ye must tread down with your feet the residue of your pastures? and to have drunk of the deep waters, but ye must foul the residue with your feet?

~EZEKIAL 34:18

Strength

THE Lord God is my strength, and he will
make my feet like hinds' feet, and he will
make me to walk upon mine high places.

~HABAKKUK 3:19

...AND when he had spoken unto me, I was
strengthened, and said, Let my lord speak;
for thou hast strengthened me.

~DANIEL 10:19

YE are the light of the world. A city that is set
on an hill cannot be hid.

~MATTHEW 5:14

THE LORD is my rock, and my fortress, and my deliverer; my God, my strength, in whom I will trust; my buckler, and the horn of my salvation, and my high tower.

~*PSALMS 18:2*

THERE hath no temptation taken you but such as is common to man: but God is faithful, who will not suffer you to be tempted above that ye are able; but will with the temptation also make a way to escape, that ye may be able to bear it.

~*1 CORINTHIANS 10:13*

THE LORD is my strength and song, and he is become my salvation: he is my God, and I will prepare him an habitation; my father's God, and I will exalt him.

~*EXODUS 15:2*

BUT be not thou far from me, O LORD: O my strength, haste thee to help me.

~PSALMS 22:19

THE LORD is my strength and my shield; my heart trusted in him, and I am helped: therefore my heart greatly rejoiceth; and with my song will I praise him.

~PSALMS 28:7

BUT I will sing of thy power; yea, I will sing aloud of thy mercy in the morning: for thou hast been my defence and refuge in the day of my trouble.

~PSALMS 59:16

Thankfulness

TO GOD

O give thanks unto the God of heaven: for his mercy endureth for ever.

~PSALMS 136:26

REJOICE evermore. Pray without ceasing. In every thing give thanks: for this is the will of God in Christ Jesus concerning you.

~1 THESSALONIANS 5:16–18

THIS is the day which the LORD hath made; we will rejoice and be glad in it.

~PSALMS 118:24

O LORD, thou hast brought up my soul from the grave: thou hast kept me alive, that I should not go down to the pit. Sing unto the LORD, O ye saints of his, and give thanks at the remembrance of his holiness. For his anger endureth but a moment; in his favour is life: weeping may endure for a night, but joy cometh in the morning.

~PSALMS 30:3–5

NOW thanks be unto God, which always causeth us to triumph in Christ, and maketh manifest the savour of his knowledge by us in every place.

~2 CORINTHIANS 2:14

BLESSED be the LORD, because he hath heard the voice of my supplications.

~ISAIAH 28:6

Giving thanks
unto the Father,
which hath made
us meet to be
partakers of the
inheritance of the
saints in light.

~COLOSSIANS 1:12

THEREFORE I will give thanks unto thee, O LORD, among the heathen, and I will sing praises unto thy name.

~2 SAMUEL 22:50

AND be not drunk with wine, wherein is excess; but be filled with the Spirit; Speaking to yourselves in psalms and hymns and spiritual songs, singing and making melody in your heart to the Lord; Giving thanks always for all things unto God and the Father in the name of our Lord Jesus Christ.

~EPHESIANS 5:18–20

THOU hast made known to me the ways of life; thou shalt make me full of joy with thy countenance.

~ACTS 2:28

Trust

PRESERVE me, O God: for in thee do I
put my trust.

~PSALMS 16:1

IN God I will praise his word, in God I have
put my trust; I will not fear what flesh can
do unto me.

~PSALMS 56:4

HE will not suffer thy foot to be moved: he
that keepeth thee will not slumber.

~PSALMS 121:3

CAUSE me to hear thy lovingkindness in the morning; for in thee do I trust: cause me to know the way wherein I should walk; for I lift up my soul unto thee.

~PSALMS 143:8

PUT not your trust in princes, nor in the son of man, in whom there is no help.

~PSALMS 146:3

CASTING all your care upon him; for he careth for you.

~1 PETER 5:7

LET your conversation be without covetousness; and be content with such things as ye have: for he hath said, I will never leave thee, nor forsake thee.

~HEBREWS 13:5

AND this is the confidence that we have in him, that, if we ask any thing according to his will, he heareth us: And if we know that he hear us, whatsoever we ask, we know that we have the petitions that we desired of him.

~2 JOHN 5:14–15

FOR we walk by faith, not by sight.

~2 CORINTHIANS 5:7

AND he said, The LORD is my rock, and my fortress, and my deliverer; The God of my rock; in him will I trust: he is my shield, and the horn of my salvation, my high tower, and my refuge, my saviour; thou savest me from violence.

~2 SAMUEL 22:2–3

Truth

AND ye shall know the truth, and the truth shall make you free.

~JOHN 8:32

THE lip of truth shall be established for ever: but a lying tongue is but for a moment.

~PROVERBS 12:19

LEAD me in thy truth, and teach me: for thou art the God of my salvation; on thee do I wait all the day.

~PSALMS 25:5

OPEN rebuke is better than secret love.

~PROVERBS 27:5

LET not mercy and truth forsake thee: bind them about thy neck; write them upon the table of thine heart.

~PROVERBS 3:3

BELOVED, believe not every spirit, but try the spirits whether they are of God: because many false prophets are gone out into the world.

~1 JOHN 4:1

THY word is true from the beginning: and every one of thy righteous judgments endureth for ever.

~PSALMS 119:160

The heart is
deceitful above
all things, and
desperately
wicked: who
can know it?

~JEREMIAH 17:9

ASK, and it shall be given you; seek,
and ye shall find; knock, and it shall be
opened unto you.

~MATTHEW 7:7

FINALLY, brethren, whatsoever things
are true, whatsoever things are honest,
whatsoever things are just, whatsoever
things are pure, whatsoever things are lovely,
whatsoever things are of good report; if there
be any virtue, and if there be any praise,
think on these things.

~PHILIPPIANS 4:8

PILATE therefore said unto him, Art thou a
king then? Jesus answered, Thou sayest that I
am a king. To this end was I born, and for this
cause came I into the world, that I should
bear witness unto the truth. Every one that is
of the truth heareth my voice.

~JOHN 18:37

Work

AND whatsoever ye do, do it heartily, as to the Lord, and not unto men.

~*COLOSSIANS 3:23*

NOT slothful in business; fervent in spirit; serving the Lord.

~*ROMANS 12:11*

FOR thou shalt eat the labour of thine hands: happy shalt thou be, and it shall be well with thee.

~*PSALMS 128:2*

IN all labour there is profit: but the talk of the lips tendeth only to penury.

~PROVERBS 14:23

COMMIT thy works unto the LORD, and thy thoughts shall be established.

~PROVERBS 16:3

I have glorified thee on the earth: I have finished the work which thou gavest me to do.

~JOHN 17:4

SIX days shall work be done: but the seventh day is the sabbath of rest, an holy convocation; ye shall do no work therein: it is the sabbath of the LORD in all your dwellings.

~LEVITICUS 23:3

THE LORD shall open unto thee his good
treasure, the heaven to give the rain unto thy
land in his season, and to bless all the work
of thine hand: and thou shalt lend unto many
nations, and thou shalt not borrow.

~DEUTERONOMY 28:12

AND that ye study to be quiet, and to do your
own business, and to work with your own
hands, as we commanded you.

~1 THESSALONIANS 4:11

...BE ye stedfast, unmoveable, always
abounding in the work of the Lord,
forasmuch as ye know that your labour is not
in vain in the Lord.

~1 CORINTHIANS 15:58

Worldly
THINGS

LOVE not the world, neither the things that are in the world. If any man love the world, the love of the Father is not in him

~1 JOHN 2:15

SET your affection on things above, not on things on the earth.

~COLOSSIANS 3:2

FOR we brought nothing into this world, and it is certain we can carry nothing out.

~1 TIMOTHY 6:7

AND be not conformed to this world: but be ye transformed by the renewing of your mind, that ye may prove what is that good, and acceptable, and perfect, will of God.

~ROMANS 12:2

AND that which fell among thorns are they, which, when they have heard, go forth, and are choked with cares and riches and pleasures of this life, and bring no fruit to perfection.

~LUKE 8:14

IF therefore ye have not been faithful in the unrighteous mammon, who will commit to your trust the true riches?

~LUKE 16:11

Teaching us that, denying ungodliness and worldly lusts, we should live soberly, righteously, and godly, in this present world.

~TITUS 2:12

LET not thine heart envy sinners: but be thou in the fear of the LORD all the day long.

~PROVERBS 23:17

AND we know that we are of God, and the whole world lieth in wickedness.

~1 JOHN 5:19

IF the world hate you, ye know that it hated me before it hated you.

~JOHN 15:18

Worship

FOR thou art my rock and my fortress;
therefore for thy name's sake lead me,
and guide me.

~PSALMS 31:3

I will pay my vows unto the LORD now in the
presence of all his people.

~PSALMS 116:14

I will bless the LORD at all times: his praise
shall continually be in my mouth. My soul
shall make her boast in the LORD: the
humble shall hear thereof, and be glad.

~PSALMS 34:1-2

O give thanks unto the LORD; call upon
his name: make known his deeds among
the people.

~PSALMS 105:1

BEWARE of false prophets, which come to
you in sheep's clothing, but inwardly they are
ravening wolves.

~MATTHEW 7:15

GLORY to God in the highest, and on earth
peace, good will toward men.

~LUKE 2:14

O Lord, thou art my God; I will exalt thee,
I will praise thy name; for thou hast done
wonderful things; thy counsels of old are
faithfulness and truth.

~ISAIAH 25:1

THINE, O LORD is the greatness, and the
power, and the glory, and the victory, and
the majesty: for all that is in the heaven and
in the earth is thine; thine is the kingdom,
O LORD, and thou art exalted as head
above all.

~1 CHRONICLES 29:11

O God, thou art my God; early will I seek
thee: my soul thirsteth for thee, my flesh
longeth for thee in a dry and thirsty land,
where no water is.

~PSALMS 63:1

WHO shall not fear thee, O Lord, and glorify thy name? for thou only art holy: for all nations shall come and worship before thee; for thy judgments are made manifest.

~REVELATIONS 15:4

AND lest thou lift up thine eyes unto heaven, and when thou seest the sun, and the moon, and the stars, even all the host of heaven, shouldest be driven to worship them, and serve them, which the LORD thy God hath divided unto all nations under the whole heaven.

~DEUTERONOMY 4:19

AND Jesus answered and said unto him, Get thee behind me, Satan: for it is written, Thou shalt worship the Lord thy God, and him only shalt thou serve.

~LUKE 4:8

Then shall ye call upon me, and ye shall go and pray unto me, and I will hearken unto you.

~JEREMIAH 29:12